1001
Jokes
for
Kids

LAUGHS FOR ALL AGES!

PETER PAUPER PRESS, INC.
White Plains, New York

PETER PAUPER PRESS

In 1928, at the age of twenty-two, Peter Beilenson began printing books on a small press in the basement of his parents' home in Larchmont, New York. Peter—and later, his wife, Edna—sought to create fine books that sold at "prices even a pauper could afford."

Today, still family owned and operated, Peter Pauper Press continues to honor our founders' legacy of quality, value, and fun for big kids and small kids alike.

Designed by Heather Zschock
Images used under license from Shutterstock.com

Copyright © 2022 Peter Pauper Press, Inc.
202 Mamaroneck Avenue
White Plains, NY 10601 USA
All rights reserved
ISBN 978-1-4413-3943-0
Printed in China

Published in the United Kingdom and Europe by
Peter Pauper Press, Inc. c/o White Pebble International
Units 2-3, Spring Business Park
Stanbridge Road
Havant, Hampshire PO9 2GJ UK

7 6 5 4 3 2 1

Visit us at www.peterpauper.com

Contents

Welcome jesters, jokesters, clowns, and wisecrackers!

Not only is laughter the best medicine, it's also just plain fun! With **1,001 Jokes for Kids**, you can keep your sense of humor with you at all times.

This book is a collection of some of the all-time funniest jokes for any occasion! Whether you're looking to laugh about school, the weather, or even toilets, we've got you covered. Pick from any of the following thousand (and one!) jokes and prepare to become everyone's favorite comedian.

A good sense of humor can help you smile in the darkest times and can make the good times even brighter! So whenever you see someone in need of a laugh, just pull out this book and treat yourself to a chuckle.

Spooky

Where do ghosts like to trick-or-treat?
Dead ends.

Where does Dracula keep his money?
In a blood bank.

What is a witch's favorite subject?
Spelling.

What do mummies listen to on Halloween?
Wrap music.

What's a monster's favorite dessert?
Leeches and scream!

Why didn't the skeleton go to prom?
He had no body to go with.

How do you make a skeleton laugh?
You tickle his funny bone.

How can you tell that vampires love baseball?
They turn into bats every night.

Where do ghosts shop for sheets?
Bootiques!

**What kind of key does a ghost use
to unlock his room?**
A spoo-key!

Why do ghosts ride elevators?
To raise their spirits.

**What do you call a witch
at the beach?**
A sand-witch!

Where can you find a monster snail?
At the end of a monster's finger.

**What do you call two witches
living together?**
Broommates!

**What do you get when you cross
a werewolf and a vampire?**
A fur coat that fangs around your neck!

**What do you call two spiders
that just got married?**
Newlywebbed!

**What do you get when you cross
a vampire with a snowman?**
Frostbite!

**What do you get when you cross
a vampire with a teacher?**
A blood test!

Why are ghosts so bad at lying?
Because you can see right through them.

**What happens when a ghost
gets lost in the fog?**
He is mist.

What is a vampire most afraid of?
Tooth decay!

How do you know if a zombie likes someone?
They ask for seconds!

What do you use to mend a jack-o-lantern?
A pumpkin patch!

What do vampires and false teeth have in common?
They both come out at night.

What do you do when a hundred monsters surround your house?
Hope that it's Halloween.

What do skeletons say before eating?
Bone appetit!

Why do cemeteries have fences?
Because people are dying to get in!

Why did the witch take a nap?
She needed to rest a spell.

Why did the zombie become a mortician?
To put food on the table.

**What's the problem with
twin witches?**

You never know witch is which!

**Why did the zombie stay home
from school?**

He felt rotten!

Why are graveyards so noisy?

Because of all the coffin!

**Who's the scariest body builder
of all time?**

Dr. Frankenstein.

What do you call a cleaning skeleton?

The grim sweeper!

What's it like to be kissed by a vampire?

It's a pain in the neck!

**What did the daddy ghost say
to the baby ghost?**

Fasten your sheet belt!

What's a zombie's favorite treat?

Eye candy.

What did the pumpkin say to the carver?
Cut it out!

What game do monsters play?
Hide and shriek.

Who won the skeleton beauty contest?
No body!

What shampoo do zombies use?
Head and Shoulders.

Why don't werewolves ever know the time?
Because they're not whenwolves.

Why was the mummy so tense?
He was all wound up!

Why do zombies make good makeup artists?
Because they have to put their face on every morning.

Why do ghosts make the best cheerleaders?
They have a lot of spirit!

Why did the skeleton start a fight?
Because he had a bone to pick!

What do you call a witch's garage?
A broom closet!

Why did the skeleton cross the road?
To get to the body shop!

Who did Frankenstein take to prom?
His ghoulfriend.

What did the zombie say to the villager?
Nice to eat you!

What's a vampire's favorite fruit?
Necktarines.

What does a shocked pumpkin say?
Oh my gourd!

What's Dracula's favorite holiday?
Fangs-giving!

What do witches put in their hair?
Scare spray.

**Do zombies eat popcorn with
their fingers?**
No, they eat their fingers separately!

What soccer position did the ghost play?
Ghoulkeeper!

Why can't Frankenstein fly?
He never makes it through the metal detector.

What's big, furry, and has eight wheels?
A monster on roller skates.

What is a ghost's favorite fruit?
Booberries!

What do you call a haunted chicken?
A poultry–geist!

What noise does a witch's cereal make?
Snap, cackle, and pop.

**What Halloween snack will keep
you up all night?**
A coffee apple!

**How do you describe a monster
with great hearing?**
Eerie!

Why didn't the zombie cross the road?
He didn't have the guts.

Why don't zombies like pirates?
They're too salty.

What happens to teen witches who break the rules?
They get ex–spelled!

What's the best thing to put into a pumpkin pie?
Your teeth!

Why don't they play music in skeleton church?
No organs!

Why did the ghost go to the yard sale?
He was a bargain haunter!

What did the vampire doctor say in the waiting room?
Necks please!

Why did the vampire read the newspaper?
He heard it had great circulation.

How do vampires get around?
On blood vessels!

How do you make a witch itch?
Take away the "w"!

What's the funniest day of the year?
Ha-halloween!

**Did you hear about the monster
who ate too many houses?**
He was homesick.

Why was the cyclops crying?
He lost his moistur-eyes-er!

Can a monster jump higher than a tree?
Of course! Trees can't jump.

**Who helped the little pumpkin
cross the road?**
The crossing gourd!

Why was the vampire stressed?
There was a lot at stake!

**Why did the headless horseman
go into business?**
He wanted to get ahead in life.

Prehistoric

**What do you call a dinosaur wearing
a cowboy hat and boots?**
Tyrannosaurus Tex!

**What should you do if you see a blue
Dilophosaurus?**
Try to cheer him up.

What do you call a dinosaur car accident?
A Tyrannosaurus wreck!

What kind of dinosaur is made of cheese?
Gorgonzilla!

What is found in the middle of dinosaurs?
The letter S!

Why does the Brontosaurus have a long neck?
Its feet smell!

**What's the best way to raise a
baby dinosaur?**
With a crane.

**What do you get if you cross a
T-rex with explosives?**

Dino–mite!

Why did the T-rex cross the road?

Because chickens hadn't evolved yet.

**What is a dinosaur's least favorite
reindeer?**

Comet!

**What does a T-rex do when it
takes you out to lunch?**

*First, it pours salt on your head.
Then, it takes out a fork.*

**What do you call a paleontologist
who naps on the job?**

Lazy bones!

Where do dinosaurs go shopping?

The dino–store.

What did dinosaurs use to drive their cars?

Fossil fuels!

What do you call a dinosaur ghost?

A scare–o–dactyl!

**What do you call a group of
dinosaurs that sing?**
A Tyranno-chorus!

**What do you call a short, spiky dinosaur
that's fallen down the stairs?**
Ankle-is-sore-us!

**What do you call a dinosaur who
has left its armor in the rain?**
A Stegosau-rust!

**Did you hear about the T-rex
who entertained a lot?**
It always had friends for lunch.

**How do you ask a Tyrannosaurus
out to lunch?**
"Tea, Rex?"

**What do you call a dinosaur you're
hiding from?**
Doyouthinkysaurus?

**What's the best thing to do
if you see a T-rex?**
Hope he doesn't see you.

**What do you get when a
dinosaur sneezes?**
Out of the way!

**What do you call a dinosaur
who is a loud sleeper?**
A Tyranno-snorus!

**What do you call a dinosaur that
never gives up?**
Try-try-try-ceratops!

What came after the dinosaurs?
Their tails.

**How do you know if a Seismosaurus
is under your bed?**
*Because your nose is only two
inches from the ceiling.*

**What would happen if a 100-ton
Brachiosaurus stepped on you?**
You'd be deeply impressed.

**What did the caveman say as he
slid down the dinosaur's neck?**
So long!

**What is a Stegosaurus's favorite
playground toy?**
A dino-see-saw-r!

How do dinosaurs apologize?
I'm-so-saurus!

**What type of tool does a prehistoric
carpenter use?**
A dino-saw.

**What's a nickname for someone who put
their right hand in the mouth of a T-rex?**
Lefty.

Do you know how long dinosaurs lived?
The same as short ones.

What do you call a T-rex wizard?
A dinosorcerer!

**What game does a Brontosaurus
like to play with humans?**
Squash.

**What did the salesperson say to
the dinosaur buying a gift?**
You want that gift raptor not?

**What did the dinosaur call her
blouse business?**
Try Sara's Tops!

What do you call twin dinosaurs?
Pair-odactyls!

**What do you get if you cross a
dinosaur with a pig?**
Jurassic Pork!

**What do you call a dinosaur
with headphones?**
Anything you like! He can't hear you.

**What do you call an anxious
dinosaur?**
A nervous rex.

**What materials do dinosaurs use
to build their homes?**
Rep-tiles.

**What do you call a T-rex that
hates losing?**
A saur loser!

**What do you call a dinosaur that
knows a lot of words?**
A thesaurus!

**When can three giant dinosaurs share
an umbrella and not get wet?**
When it's not raining.

What's the best way to talk to a Velociraptor?
Long-distance!

Why didn't the caveman cross the road?
Roads hadn't been invented yet.

Why are dinosaurs extinct?
Because they wouldn't take a bath!

**What did one paleontologist
say to the other?**
I've got a bone to pick with you!

Why did the Apatosaurus devour the factory?
She was a plant-eater.

**What do you call a dinosaur that
asks a lot of questions?**
A philosiraptor!

How can you tell if there's an Amargasaurus in your bed?

The bright red "A" on its pajamas.

What happened when the Brachiosaurus took the train home?

He had to bring it back!

What kind of dinosaur can you ride in a rodeo?

A Bronco-saurus!

How many dinosaurs can you fit in an empty box?

One—after that, it's not empty!

What did the dinosaur say when he saw the volcano explode?

What a lavaly day!

Why should you never ask a Diplodocus to read you a story?

Because their tales are so long.

Why was the Stegosaurus so good at volleyball?

It could really spike the ball!

What does a dinosaur call a porcupine?
A toothbrush!

What's as big as a dinosaur but weighs nothing?
A dinosaur's shadow.

What comes after extinction?
Y-stinction.

What comes after Y-stinction?
Z-end!

Why can't dinosaurs go on cruises?
They cause too many ship rex!

What do you call a caveman's fart?
A blast from the past.

What do you call a beautiful dinosaur?
A sight for saur eyes!

What do you get when a dinosaur walks through a strawberry patch?
Strawberry jam!

**What weighs 800 pounds and sticks
to the roof of your mouth?**
A peanut butter and Stegosaurus sandwich!

Why did the Archaeopteryx catch the worm?
It was an early bird.

**Why can't you hear a Pterodactyl
going to the bathroom?**
Because the pee is silent!

**What do you call someone who just won't
stop talking about prehistoric creatures?**
A dino-bore!

**Can you name 10 dinosaurs in
10 seconds?**
Yes! 8 Triceratops and 2 Stegosaurus.

**Why did carnivorous dinosaurs
eat raw meat?**
Because they didn't have a barbecue grill.

**How can you tell when there's a
Thalassomedon in your refrigerator?**
The door won't close!

**What makes more noise than
a baby dinosaur?**
Two baby dinosaurs!

**What should you do if you spot
a Liopleurodon?**
Start swimming!

What prehistoric animal was the scariest?
The terror-dactyl!

What do you call a dino in high heels?
My-feet-are-saurus.

**How did cavemen survive the asteroid
that killed the dinosaurs?**
*They kept their distance and were
65 million years apart.*

Why do museums display old dinosaur bones?
They can't afford new ones.

What does a Triceratops sit on?
Its tricera-bottom!

Weather & Nature

How do you prevent a summer cold?
Catch it in the winter.

What did one lightning bolt say to the other?
You're shocking!

What did one thermometer say to the other?
You make my temperature rise!

How did the cat know about tomorrow's weather?
He looked at the fur-cast.

How do leaves get from place to place?
They use autumn-mobiles.

Where do snowmen keep their money?
In a snow bank!

What weather is most striking?
Lightning!

What is so lazy that it never gets up?
Fog!

Why did the lightning get in trouble?
It couldn't conduct itself.

**Why do bananas need a lot of
sunscreen at the beach?**
They peel!

How does a thunderstorm catch fish?
With a lightning rod.

What is the opposite of a cold front?
A warm back.

What did the tree say to spring?
What a re-leaf!

**Who does everyone listen to,
but no one believes?**
The weather reporter!

What falls but never hits the ground?
The temperature.

What do snowmen call their kids?
Chill-dren!

When do monkeys fall from the sky?
During Ape-ril showers!

**What do you do in the summer
in the North Pole?**
If it comes on a weekend, you have a picnic.

Why can't a dust storm be a comedian?
Its sense of humor is too dry.

**Did you hear about the cow that
was swept away by a tornado?**
It was an udder disaster.

**Where can you find an ocean
without any water?**
On a map!

When are your eyes not eyes?
When the cold wind makes them water.

Did you hear the story of the tornado?
There's a twist at the end!

What did the hat say to the scarf?
You hang around while I go on ahead!

What did the tornado say to the sports car?
Wanna go for a spin?

**How do you find the weather when
you're on vacation?**
Go outside and look up.

**What happens when the fog lifts
in California?**
UCLA!

**Did you hear about the bed bugs
who fell in love?**
They're getting married in the spring!

Why does the farmer hate picking vegetables?
It's the harvest part.

**What do you say before it
rains candy?**
It sprinkles!

**Why can't you write a novel
about a small garden?**

There's not much of a plot!

What music do wind turbines listen to?

They're huge metal fans.

**Why couldn't the woman plant
any flowers?**
She hadn't botany!

**What do you call it when it's pouring
ducks and geese?**
Fowl weather!

Can February March?
No, but April May!

What eight letters can you find in the water?
H to O!

Why would you meditate during a storm?
It's an in-lightening experience.

**What do you get when you pour hot water
down a rabbit hole?**
A hot cross bunny!

What did one raindrop say to the other?
Two's company. Three's a cloud.

How do thunderstorms invest their money?
In liquid assets!

What do you call an old snowman?
Water!

Why is it tough to grow an herb garden?
It's hard to find thyme for it.

What did one AC unit say to the other?
I'm your biggest fan!

**How do you win the grand prize at
the weather forecasting competition?**
You beat the raining champion.

**You're locked in a room with only a bed
and a calendar. How do you survive?**
You eat the dates and drink from the springs.

Why shouldn't you start a fight with a cloud?
He'll storm out on you!

Why did the tornado take a break?
It was out of wind.

What's the best way to make a tree laugh?
Tell it acorn-y joke!

Why did the woman buy potting soil on sale?
It was dirt cheap.

What do trees say when they get cut down?
I'm stumped.

What's a trampoline's favorite season?
Spring-time!

**What's the difference between a horse
and the weather?**
One is reined up and the other rains down.

What vegetable is forbidden on ships?
Leeks!

**How do you stop your newspaper from
flying away in a dust storm?**
Use a news anchor.

What happens when winter arrives?
Autumn leaves!

What do you call a nosy tree?
A leaves-dropper!

What did the snowman put over his baby's crib?

A snowmobile!

What is a mountain's favorite type of candy?

Snow caps!

Why did the woman go outside with her purse open?

Because she expected some change in the weather.

What do you call a cold ghost?

Casp-brr!

What's worse than raining buckets?

Hailing taxis!

What's a forest's favorite school subject?

Geometree.

Why did the gardener move back to his hometown?

To rediscover his roots.

Where do clouds go the bathroom?

Anywhere they want!

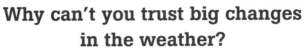

What did the tree say to autumn?
Leaf me alone!

Why can't you trust big changes in the weather?
It's just a front!

What do you call 60 seconds in 90-degree weather?
A hot minute.

How did the gardener brighten his garden?
He planted some bulbs!

How do trees get online?
They just log in.

What looks like half a pine tree?
The other half!

How do you identify a dogwood tree?
By the bark.

How do you cut a wave in half?
Use a sea saw.

What did one tide pool say to the other?
Show me your mussels!

**What's the difference between
weather and climate?**
You can't weather a tree, but you can climate.

**What does a cloud wear under
his raincoat?**
Thunderwear!

What did the fog say to the valley?
I mist you!

What goes up when the rain comes down?
An umbrella!

How do hurricanes see?
With one eye.

What's a tornado's favorite game?
Twister.

**Why did the evergreen tree write
a love letter?**
It was pining.

History

**Who succeeded the first President
of the United States?**

The second one.

**Who succeeded the second President
of the United States?**

The third one. (Gotcha!)

What do you call a vegan Viking?

Norvegan!

**Which famous Roman suffered
from hay fever?**

Julius Sneezer!

**What do William the Conqueror and
Kermit the Frog have in common?**

They have the same middle name.

Why did Henry VIII struggle to breathe?

He had no heir.

How did Vikings send secret messages?

By Norse code!

What was written on a knight's headstone?

Rust in peace!

Why did the pioneers cross the United States in wagons?

Because they didn't want to wait forty years for a train.

Which English royal family was the smartest?

The Tudors.

Did you hear the joke about the Liberty Bell?

It cracked me up!

How do you become good at making Greek pottery?

You have to urn it.

Where do young Vikings hang out?

In the Norsery!

What did medieval post officers wear?

Chain mail.

Why did King Arthur have a round table?

So nobody could corner him.

When did George Washington die?
Just before they buried him!

**What's the most popular kids'
movie in Ancient Greece?**
Troy Story!

**Archaeologists recently discovered a statue of
a pink lady in a T–Bird. What did they call it?**
Ancient Grease.

**What would you get if you crossed the
American national bird with Snoopy?**
A bald beagle!

**Where did the pilgrims land when
they came to America?**
On their feet.

How was the Roman Empire cut in half?
With a pair of Caesars!

What's purple and 5,000 miles long?
The grape wall of China.

**Two wrongs don't make a right,
but what do two Wrights make?**
An airplane!

Why was the king only a foot tall?
Because he was a ruler!

Why did Julius Caesar need crayons?
He wanted to mark Antony.

If Atlas supported the world on his shoulders, who supported Atlas?
His family and friends.

Why didn't the Romans need to study algebra?
Because X always equaled 10.

Why did Paul Revere ride his horse from Boston to Lexington?
Because the horse was too heavy to carry.

What did Isaac Newton's doctor tell him when the apple fell on his head?
I don't think you understand the gravity of this situation.

What was the most popular dance move in America in 1776?
Indepen-dance!

Who was the biggest prankster in George Washington's army?
Laugh–ayette!

What do you call a knight who's always sure of himself?
Sir Tainly.

Who built King Arthur's round table?
Sir Cumference!

What did they do at the Boston Tea Party?
I don't know, I wasn't invited!

What was the Romans' greatest achievement?
Learning to speak Latin.

Why did the Vikings sail to England in longboats?
It was too far to swim.

Why is the medieval period called the Dark Ages?
Because there were so many knights!

What was George Washington's favorite tree?
The infantry!

What did one turkey say to the other when they saw the pilgrims?

They look nice. Maybe they'll have us over for dinner.

What did Caesar say to Cleopatra?

Toga-ther we can rule the world.

What happened when the student failed her Revolutionary War exam?

She went down in History.

The Declaration of Independence was written in Philadelphia: True or false?

False! It was written in ink.

Who invented fractions?

Henry the 1/8th!

What did the Statue of Liberty say after leaving a party?

Keep in torch!

What was Camelot?

A place to park camels.

What does the Statue of Liberty stand for?

Because it can't sit down!

What kind of tea did the American colonists want at the Boston Tea Party?

Liberty!

Where was the Declaration of Independence signed?

At the bottom.

Why did Renoir become an Impressionist?

He did it for the Monet.

What did the colonists do because of the Stamp Act?

They licked the British!

Why did the knight run around shouting for a can opener?

He had a bumblebee in his suit of armor!

What was the most groundbreaking invention in human history?

The shovel.

Who was Socrates's worst student?

Mediocrities.

**What did King George think
of the American colonies?**
He found them revolting.

**What's big, cracked, and carries
your luggage?**
The Liberty Bellhop!

**Why did George Washington have
trouble sleeping?**
Because he couldn't lie.

**How did Louis XIV feel after completing
the Palace of Versailles?**
Baroque.

Why was Socrates's star student so busy?
He had a lot on his Plato.

**Which explorer was the best
at hide-and-seek?**
Marco Polo!

Who yelled, "Coming are British the"?
Paul Reverse.

Where do pirates keep their bathrooms?
On the poop deck!

What do pirates put on their toast?
Jelly Roger!

**Why couldn't the pirate king
play cards?**
Because he was standing on the deck.

**What's the difference between a pirate
and a cranberry farmer?**
*The pirate buries his treasure,
and the farmer treasures his berries.*

Which pirate has the biggest hat?
The one with the biggest head.

What would you call a pirate with no eye?
A prate.

**What would you call a pirate
with four eyes?**
A piiiirate!

Where do pirates put their weapons?
In their enemies.

**Why does it take pirates so long
to learn the alphabet?**
Because they spend years at C.

Where did Caesar keep his armies?
Up his sleevies!

The pilgrims' cows came to America on what ship?
The Mooooo-flower.

Why didn't the settlers take turkeys to church?
They used fowl language!

What did the pilgrims use to bake cookies?
May-flour!

What kind of music did the pilgrims like?
Plymouth Rock!

If pilgrims were alive today, what would they be most famous for?
Their age.

How did Benjamin Franklin feel when he discovered electricity?
Shocked!

What is red, white, blue, and yellow?
A star-spangled banana!

Toilet Humor

Why do people fall asleep on the toilet?
Because they're in the restroom.

How does a clown fart smell?
Pretty funny!

What did the doctor say when her patient got a bladder infection?
"I see urine trouble."

What did she say when the infection was cured?
"I see urine luck!"

What do you call a fairy on the toilet?
Stinker Bell!

Why did the toilet paper roll down the hill?
To make it to the bottom.

**Why couldn't the police officers
find the toilet thief?**
Because they had nothing to go on!

**Why didn't the toilet paper make
it across the road?**
It got stuck in the crack.

**How many people does it take to
make the bathroom smell?**
Just a phew!

What's a toilet's favorite sport?
Bowl-ing!

Why did the baker's hands stink?
He kneaded a poo.

Why does Superman always flush the toilet?
Because it's his doody!

Why did the baby put quarters in its diaper?
It needed to be changed!

**If pooping is the call of nature,
what's farting?**
A missed call.

What happened on the toilet's birthday?
A surprise potty!

What do you call a dog that you find in your bathroom?
A poodle!

What do octopuses do after using the toilet?
They wash their hands, hands, hands, hands, hands, hands, hands, hands.

Why did the toilet sleep late?
He was feeling a little wiped!

When do you need to buy a new toilet?
When the one you have is full.

Why do ducks have so many feathers?
To cover up their butt quacks!

Why did the comedian with diarrhea cancel his gig last minute?
Sometimes that kind of thing falls through.

What do you do if you find a bear using your bathroom?
You let it finish!

Why was Tigger in the bathroom?
He was looking for Pooh!

**Why didn't the man take his phone
into the bathroom?**
He didn't want to give away his IP address.

**What are two reasons you shouldn't
drink toilet water?**
Easy, number 1 and number 2.

What did the poop say to the fart?
Wow, you really blow me away!

**If you're an American in the living room,
what are you in the bathroom?**
Euro-pee-an!

What happens if you fall into the toilet?
You either stink or swim!

Where do sheep like to play?
The baaa-throom.

What did one toilet say to the other?
You look a little flushed!

What are the king's farts called?
Noble gases.

What do you get when you poop in your overalls?
Dung-arees.

How do you unlock a toilet when you're in a hurry?
You use a doo-key!

Did you ever hear about the movie "Constipated"?
It never came out!

Did you hear about the sequel, "Diarrhea"?
It leaked, so they released it early.

Do you know the difference between toilet paper and a shower curtain?
(Wait for a "no" response.)
So you're the one!

What do you call a poop magician?
Poo-dini.

Why do some banks not have toilets?
Because not all banks accept deposits.

Why was the constipated accountant fired?
He could not budget.

**Which poop movie in a trilogy
is the worst of all?**
The turd one!

Why do people hate poop jokes?
They kind of stink!

What did one fly say to the other?
"Is this stool taken?"

Where do bees go to the bathroom?
The BP station.

**What do you get when you cross
a rhino and a toilet?**
No idea, but I'm not using that bathroom.

When is the best time to use the bathroom?
Poo-thirty!

What's brown and sticky?
A stick!

Why was the toilet seat crying?
He just got dumped!

Why did they fire the constipated composer?
He was having problems with his last movement.

**What's the difference between
good and bad toilet paper?**
One is terrible, and one is tearable.

What do you call a planet that poops?
Uranus.

**What do politicians and diapers
have in common?**
They both need to be changed often.

**Why do doctors say 4 out of 5 people
suffer from diarrhea?**
Because one guy likes it.

**What do you get if you eat four
cans of alphabet soup?**
A good vowel movement.

Why did the chicken cross the road?
The chicken next to him farted.

What's funnier: jokes about healthy poop, or diarrhea?
Diarrhea. The others are a solid number 2.

What do dung beetles eat while watching a movie?
Poopcorn!

What's something you never appreciate until it's gone?
Toilet paper.

What's the German word for constipation?
Farfrompoopen.

Why should you tell your friends poop jokes?
They really get the potty started!

Why did the man bring toilet paper to the party?
He's a potty pooper!

Why don't farts graduate high school?
Because they always end up getting expelled!

Fantasy

Why did Cinderella lose the soccer game?

Because she ran away from the ball.

What do elves learn in school?

The elf–abet!

Why don't mermaids play tennis?

They might get caught in the net.

What did the wizard do when he got tired?

He sat down for a spell.

How did Jack know how many beans his cow was worth?

He used a cowculator!

Jack stole a golden harp from the giant. Why couldn't he play it?

Because it took a lot of pluck.

What do you call a scary unicorn that comes out after dark?

A nightmare.

Why did Robin Hood steal from the rich?
*Because the poor didn't have
anything worth stealing.*

**What's beautiful, gray, and wears
glass slippers?**
Cinderellephant!

**How does a mermaid make friends
with a dolphin?**
On porpoise!

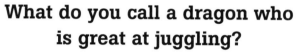

**What do you call a dragon who
is great at juggling?**
Talon-ted.

**What's a hungry dragon's favorite
day of the week?**
Chewsday!

Why are fairies so happy?
They've got great elf-help books.

**How did Little Red Riding Hood figure out
the big, bad wolf wasn't her grandma?**
*Instead of a basket of cookies,
the wolf asked for three little pigs!*

**Why was the mermaid
embarrassed?**
Because she saw the ship's bottom.

**On which side of the house did Jack
grow his magic beans?**
On the outside!

What did the beanstalk say to Jack?
Stop picking on me!

**What has beautiful hair, two arms,
a fish's tail, looks like a mermaid,
but isn't one?**
A photo of a mermaid.

**How do we know that Rapunzel
went to a lot of parties?**
Because she liked to let her hair down!

**What do you call it when a unicorn
wakes up for a midnight snack?**
Star grazing.

What do you call a philosophical fairy?
Thinker Bell.

**Why did the dinosaurs live longer
than the dragons?**

Because they didn't smoke.

Why did the mermaid ride a seahorse?

Because she was playing water polo!

What goes MUF OF EIF IF?

A giant walking backward.

**What would you call a golden egg
in a frying pan?**

An unidentified frying object!

What is higher than a giant?

A giant's hat!

**What is the difference between
Jack and the dead giant?**

One has beans, and the other is a has-been.

**Why do dragons sleep during
the day?**

So they can fight knights!

What's Snow White's brother's name?
Egg White! Get the yolk?

What's that story where the girl steals from the rich and gives it all to her granny?
Little Red Robin Hood.

What did the Ugly Duckling become after it was five days old?
Six days old.

Why did the chicken lay golden eggs?
Because if she dropped them they would dent the floor.

Which princess knows the most dad jokes?
Ra-pun-zel!

What did the unicorn say when it fell?
I've fallen and I can't giddyup.

Why are dragons so good at making music?
They really know their scales.

Why did the mermaid swim across the ocean?
To get to the other tide!

What does the frog prince eat with his hamburgers?

French flies!

Do mermaids use knives and forks when they eat?

No, they use their fish fingers!

How can you tell how much a mermaid weighs?

You check the scales!

How did Robin Hood tie his shoelaces?

With a long bow!

I want to make a really long, bad lizard joke

...but I don't want to let it dragon.

What's the tooth fairy's favorite thing about her smartphone?

She can connect it to Bluetooth.

What has a pile of gold, four legs, four wings, and a tail?

A dragon with spare parts.

Why did the dragon stop fighting with knights?

He was tired of canned food!

Where did the fisherman and mermaid meet?

On line!

Did you hear about the unicorn with a negative attitude?

She always said neigh.

Why did the unicorn get sent to bed without dinner?

She wouldn't stop horsing around at the table.

What do unicorns call their fathers?

Pop-corn!

What do you say to a three-headed ogre?

Hello, how are you today? Hello, how are you today? Hello, how are you today?

What's the difference between a unicorn and a carrot?

One is a funny beast and the other is a bunny feast.

Who granted the fish a wish?
The fairy codmother!

Why did Goldilocks have trouble sleeping?
She kept having night-bears.

What do you get when you cross chocolate powder and a dragon?
Cocoa puffs.

What steps did Goldilocks take when bears were chasing her?
Very big ones!

What do you give an ogre with great big feet?
Lots of space.

What did Cinderella say when she lost her photographs?
Someday my prints will come!

Do all fairy tales begin with "once upon a time"?
No...some begin with "If I am elected"!

**Why were the giant's fingers
only eleven inches long?**

*Because if they were twelve inches long,
they'd be a foot!*

What was Bigfoot growing in the garden?

Sas-squash.

**What do you call a pretty girl
with a broom?**

Sweeping Beauty!

**What would you get if you crossed Bo Peep's
littlest sheep with a karate expert?**

Lamb chops.

What's a fairy's favorite drink?

Sprite!

Why didn't Goldilocks eat all her porridge?

Because it was un-bear-able!

School

Why are you failing your history class?
Because the teacher keeps asking about things that happened before you were born!

How many letters are in the alphabet?
11, T-H-E-A-L-P-H-A-B-E-T!

Why are fish so smart?
Because they live in schools!

Where did the pencil go on vacation?
Pennsylvania.

Why did the laptop sneeze?
It had a virus.

Why is 2+2=5 like your left foot?
It's not right.

Why did the computer cross the road?
To get a byte to eat!

Why did the teacher jump into the pool?
He wanted to test the water.

What is the sweetest class in school?
History, because it's full of dates!

What is a snake's favorite subject in school?
Hisssssstory!

How do bees get to school?
By school buzz.

How do fish get to school?
By octobus.

What do you get when you cross one principal with another principal?
I wouldn't try, principals don't like to be crossed!

What should you do if a teacher rolls her eyes at you?
Pick them up and roll them back to her.

Why did the dog do so well in school?
Because he was the teacher's pet.

What object is king of the classroom?
The ruler!

Why do magicians do so well on exams?
They're great at trick questions.

**What's the difference between
a teacher and a train?**
*The teacher says "spit out your gum,"
and the train says "choo-choo."*

Why did the cyclops close his school?
He only had one pupil!

Why is it dangerous to do math in the jungle?
*Because when you add four and four
you get ate.*

Why can't you take an exam in the savannah?
Because there are too many cheetahs!

Why did the egg get thrown out of class?
He kept cracking yolks.

**What school requires you to drop
out in order to graduate?**
Skydiving school.

**Why was the music teacher not
able to open her classroom?**
Because her keys were on the piano!

What did the triangle say to the circle?
You're pointless!

What is a math teacher's favorite dessert?
Apple pi.

What did the paper say to the pencil?
Write on!

What did the buffalo say at school drop-off?
Bison!

Where do surfers go to school?
Boarding school.

Why did the student steal a chair from the classroom?
His teacher told him to take a seat.

What do you call a computer superhero?
A screen saver!

What flies around the school at night?
The alpha-bat.

Why did the echo get detention?
It kept talking back.

**What did the ghost teacher
say to his class?**

Look at the board and I'll go through it again!

Why is glue so bad at math?

It always gets stuck on the problems.

**What's worse than finding a
worm in your apple?**

Finding half a worm.

**Where should you grow flowers
in school?**

In the kinder-garden!

**What letter of the alphabet has
the most water?**

C!

Why did the jellybean go to school?

To become a smartie.

**What do librarians take with them
when they go fishing?**

Bookworms!

How do you make seven even?

Take away the "s"!

Why did the student bring scissors to school?

Because he wanted to cut class!

Why is math such hard work?

You have to carry all those numbers.

Why did the boy eat his homework?

His dog was busy!

**Why did student grades drop
after the holidays?**

Because everything was marked down.

**Why was the voice teacher
so good at baseball?**

Because he had perfect pitch.

Why did the computer get glasses?

To improve its website.

Why did the student bring a ladder to school?

He wanted to go to high school!

What does a book do in the winter?

It puts on a jacket.

Why did the clock in the cafeteria run slow?

It always went back four seconds!

**What did the pencil sharpener
say to the pencil?**

Stop going in circles and get to the point!

Where do math teachers go on vacation?

Times Square!

Why did the kid cross the playground?

To get to the other slide.

**What does a thesaurus eat
for breakfast?**

A synonym roll!

What are students' three favorite words?

June, July, and August.

**What time is it when Godzilla
gets to school?**

Time to run!

Why did the teacher draw on the window?

He wanted his lesson to be super clear.

What school teaches you how to greet people?

High school.

What do you call a square that's been in an accident?

A wreck-tangle!

Why did the students study in the airplane?

Because they wanted higher grades.

What kind of math do birds like?

Owl-gebra!

Why did the clock go to the principal's office?

For tocking too much!

Why was the math book sad?

Because it had so many problems.

Outer Space

**Why did the astronaut break up
with her boyfriend?**

Because she needed some space.

**Where does an astronaut
park his spaceship?**

At a parking meteor!

What do you call a white and fluffy alien?

A martian-mallow!

**What did the doctor say to
the rocket ship?**

Time to get your booster shot.

What was the first animal in space?

The cow that jumped over the moon.

What do you win in a space talent show?

A constellation prize!

What do you call a comet wrapped in bacon?
A meateor.

What did the alien say to the garden?
Take me to your weeder!

What did the alien say to the cat?
Take me to your litter!

How do you put an alien baby to sleep?
You rocket.

**Why weren't the astronauts hungry
when they got to space?**
They had a big launch.

Who was the first bug in space?
Buzz Aldrin.

Why did the cow go to outer space?
To visit the Milky Way.

Why did the moon break up with the sun?
*He never wanted to go out with
her at night!*

**What do you call
croissants in space?**
Spacetries.

**What do you get when you cross
a lamb and a rocket?**
A space sheep!

Why couldn't the star stay focused?
It kept spacing out.

Why did the alien go to Saturn?
To go ring shopping!

How did the alien break his phone?
He Saturn it.

What do you call an alien's pet?
An extra fur-restrial.

**How do you know when the moon
has had enough to eat?**
It's full!

**Where do you get change in
the solar system?**
*The moon, because it keeps
changing quarters.*

What do planets like to read?

Comet books!

**Why does nobody trust the man
on the moon?**

He has a dark side.

**Why does Jupiter have a
werewolf problem?**

It has 64 moons.

**What should you do when you
see a green alien?**

Wait until it's ripe!

**Why is Saturn the best name
for a planet?**

It's got a nice ring to it.

**What did Neil Armstrong say when no one
laughed at his moon jokes?**

I guess you had to be there.

**What did the earth make fun of
the moon for?**

Having no life.

What's loud, crunchy, and goes to space?
A rocket chip!

Where do planets go to study?
Univers–ity!

What did the moon say to the sun?
You look hot.

What do aliens do after they get married?
Go on their honeyearth.

Why is life on Earth so expensive?
*It includes a free trip around
the sun every year.*

**What do space cowboys use
to wrangle their cattle?**
A tractor beam.

**What did the astronaut say when he saw
bones on the moon?**
Obviously, the cow didn't make it.

**What happened to the alien
who stepped in gum?**
He got stuck in orbit.

What do you call a lazy man in space?
A procrastonaut.

Why would space be a popular tourist spot?
The view is breathtaking and leaves you speechless.

What happens when astronauts misbehave?
They get grounded!

What is E.T. short for?
He has little legs.

Why can't you put an observatory in your house?
The cost is astronomical!

Which is closer, Florida or the moon?
The moon. You can't see Florida from here!

How do you get clean in outer space?
You take a meteor shower!

What's a light-year?
The same as a regular year, but with less calories.

What do you do when you see a spaceman?
Park in it, man!

What's an astronaut's favorite key on the keyboard?
The space bar!

Why did Venus have to get an air conditioner?
Because Mercury moved in!

What's the difference between an astronaut and a skydiver?
Well, one is more down to earth.

What did the astronaut do after he crashed into the moon?
He Apollo-gized.

What do you get when you cross Santa Claus with a spaceship?
A U-F-Ho Ho Ho!

What do papers do when an astronaut dies?
They run an orbituary.

What happened when the rocket didn't do its work?
It got fired.

Why is there no air in space?
Because the Milky Way would go bad.

What do aliens drink when it's chilly?
Gravi-tea!

**Why was the Martian looking
for a bigger kitchen?**
He didn't have enough shelf space.

**What did the humans think of
the alien birthday party?**
It was out of this world!

**What comes from outer space
and does magic tricks?**
A flying sorcerer.

**Why haven't aliens visited
our solar system yet?**
The reviews only had one star.

What's in the center of the universe?
The letters V and E!

**If athletes get athlete's foot,
what do astronauts get?**
Missile-toe!

What kind of a star wears sunglasses?

A movie star!

What kind of dishes do they use in space?

Flying saucers.

Why didn't the sun go to university?

Because she already had a million degrees.

What's it like to eat at a restaurant on Mercury?

The food is tasty, but there's not much atmosphere!

Why don't aliens eat clowns?

Because they taste funny.

What does Mars hold up its pants with?

An asteroid belt!

Why is Earth glad to be so far away from Jupiter?

Because Jupiter is so gassy.

What did Mars say to Saturn?
Give me a ring sometime!

Why does Uranus have lots of friends?
Because it's SO cool!

What kind of songs do planets sing?
Nep-tunes.

How do you organize a party in space?
You planet.

What do you call a peanut in space?
An astronut!

When do astronauts eat?
At launch time!

How does the astronaut cut his hair?
Eclipse it.

**What is an astronaut's favorite
social network?**
Space-book!

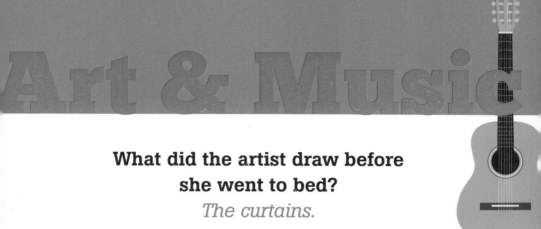

**What did the artist draw before
she went to bed?**
The curtains.

Why was music coming from the printer?
The paper was jamming.

**Why did the pianist bang his head
against the keys?**
He was playing by ear!

Why did the paintbrush see a doctor?
It had a stroke.

What famous painting is always sad?
The Moaning Lisa.

**What happened when a red ship
collided with a blue ship?**
Both of the crews were marooned.

How do you inspire an artist?
Easel-y!

Why was the artist afraid he might go to jail?
Because he'd been framed!

Why did the paintbrush make a follow-up appointment with the doctor?
It was still in paint.

What did the mama color wheel say to the baby color wheel?
Don't use that tone with me!

What do you call clean music?
A soap opera!

What has a hundred feet and sings?
A choir.

What's the difference between a fish and a piano?
You can tuna piano, but you can't tuna fish.

What do you call someone who spends 75% of their time playing football and 25% of their time playing baroque music?
A quarterbach.

What does a painter do when she feels cold?
She puts on another coat.

**What happened when two painters
entered the art contest?**
It ended in a draw.

Why did the artist get angry?
He wasn't in the right frame of mind!

Why was the artist arrested?
*Because he had an unfortunate
brush with the law.*

Why was the musician arrested?
Because she got in treble.

What do you call a set of musical dentures?
Falsetto teeth!

Why do artists make such good friends?
They always give you a shoulder to crayon.

What's green and smells like blue paint?
Green paint!

What does Salvador Dalí have for breakfast?
A bowl of surreal!

When should you fix a painting?
When it's baroque.

Want to hear the joke about a staccato?
Never mind, it's too short.

Want to hear the one about the fermata?
Wait, it's too long.

What type of music are balloons afraid of?
Pop music.

What part of a chicken is the most musical?
The drumstick!

**Why don't mathematicians
become painters?**
Their art is derivative.

**Did you hear about the artist who
took things too far?**
He didn't know where to draw the line.

**What do a sword and a piano
have in common?**
They can both B sharp!

How do you calm a piano down?

Tell it to B natural.

Why are great artists so famous?

They can always draw a crowd.

What did the robbers take from the music store?

The lute!

Why are origami artists so bad at poker?

They are always folding.

How many art gallery visitors does it take to change a lightbulb?

Two. One to do it and one to say his toddler could've done it.

What do angry painters do?

Make a scene.

How do you make a bandstand?

Take away their chairs!

What do you call a cow that plays guitar?

A moosician!

**When an artist meets his rival,
what does he say?**
I'm challenging you to a doodle.

**Why did the artist need to use
the bathroom?**
Because he was consti-painted!

What do you call a piece of art made by a cat?
A paw-trait!

**Why does everyone usually
paint Easter eggs?**
*Because it's much easier than
wallpapering them.*

**Why did the bald artist paint
rabbits on his head?**
*Because they look like hares
from a distance!*

When do artists pass away?
When they draw their last breath.

**How many conductors does it take
to change a lightbulb?**
Only one, but it takes four movements.

What has a neck, but no head?
A bass.

What's an avocado's favorite kind of music?
Guac and roll!

What makes music on your hair?
A headband!

Why did the artist hate drawing skies?
Because every time she tried, she blue it.

What did the car-painter and the carpenter say when they met?
You sound just like me!

What would you call a 15th-century Renaissance painter if he was a crab?
Leonardo da Pinchy!

What's big and gray with horns?
An elephant in a marching band.

Why can't you spot an artist in a crowd?
They're very skilled at blending in.

What always makes a painter laugh?
Sketch comedy.

**What do artists say when
they greet each other?**
Yellow!

Why did the self-portrait artist give up?
Because it just wasn't her.

**One day, I'd like to commission an artist
to make a bust of me...**
but that's getting ahead of myself.

**What do you get when you cross
a sweet potato and a jazz musician?**
A yam session!

What's a golfer's favorite genre of music?
Swing!

What key does a cow sing in?
Beef flat!

Why did Mozart get rid of his chickens?

They kept saying Bach, Bach!

Why couldn't the athlete listen to her music?

Because she just broke the record!

How do you fix a broken tuba?

With a tuba glue!

What do you get when you drop a piano on an army base?

A flat major.

What do you get when you drop a piano down a mine shaft?

A flat miner.

What makes songs, but never sings?

Notes!

Knock Knock Jokes

Knock, knock
Who's there?
Leon
Leon who?
Leon me when you're not strong!

Knock, knock
Who's there?
Annie
Annie who?
Annie thing you can do I can do better!

Knock, knock
Who's there?
Quiche
Quiche who?
Can I have a hug and a quiche?

Knock, knock
Who's there?
Harry
Harry who?
Harry up and let me in!

Knock, knock
Who's there?
Lena
Lena who?
Lena little closer, and I'll tell
you another joke!

Knock, knock
Who's there?
Avenue
Avenue who?
Avenue knocked on this door before?

Knock, knock
Who's there?
Wooden shoe
Wooden shoe who?
Wooden shoe like to
hear more jokes?

Knock, knock
Who's there?
Ice cream soda
Ice cream soda who?
Ice cream soda people can hear me!

Knock, knock
Who's there?
Nicholas
Nicholas who?
A Nicholas not much money
these days.

Knock, knock
Who's there?
A roach
A roach who?
A roach you a text, didn't you get it?

Knock, knock
Who's there?
A herd
A herd who?
A herd you were home,
so here I am!

Knock, knock
Who's there?
Wa
Wa who?
What are you so excited about?

Knock, knock
Who's there?
Interrupting pirate
Interrupting pira—
ARRRRRRRRGH

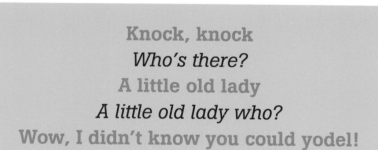

Knock, knock
Who's there?
A little old lady
A little old lady who?
Wow, I didn't know you could yodel!

Knock, knock
Who's there?
Figs
Figs who?
Figs the doorbell,
it's not working!

Knock, knock
Who's there?
Wendy
Wendy who?
Wendy bell works again,
I won't have to knock!

Knock, knock
Who's there?
Alec
Alec who?
Alec it when you ask me questions.

Knock, knock
Who's there?
Candice
Candice who?
Candice door open or am
I stuck out here?

Knock, knock
Who's there?
Sarah
Sarah who?
Is Sarah phone I could use?

Knock, knock
Who's there?
Annie
Annie who?
Annie one you like!

Knock, knock
Who's there?
A leaf
A leaf who?
A leaf you alone if you
leaf me alone.

Knock, knock
Who's there?
Luke.
Luke who?
Luke through the peephole
and find out!

Knock, knock
Who's there?
Anita
Anita who?
Anita drink of water, let me in!

Knock, knock
Who's there?
CD
CD who?
CD person on your doorstep?

Knock, knock
Who's there?
Spell
Spell who?
W-H-O!

Knock, knock
Who's there?
Watson
Watson who?
Watson TV right now?

Knock, knock
Who's there?
Tank.
Tank who?
You're welcome!

Knock, knock
Who's there?
Cash
Cash who?
No thanks, but I'd love some peanuts!

Knock, knock
Who's there?
Theodore
Theodore who?
Theodore wasn't open so I knocked!

Knock, knock
Who's there?
Candice
Candice who?
Candice joke get any worse?!

Knock, knock
Who's there?
Ivor
Ivor who?
**Ivor you let me in or I'm climbing
through the window!**

Knock, knock
Who's there?
A broken pencil
A broken pencil who?
Never mind, it's pointless.

Knock, knock
Who's there?
Honeybee
Honeybee who?
Honeybee a dear and get
the door for me!

Knock, knock
Who's there?
Ketchup
Ketchup who?
Ketchup with me and I'll tell you!

Knock, knock
Who's there?
Haven
Haven who?
Haven you heard enough of these
knock-knock jokes?

Knock, knock
Who's there?
Abbot
Abbot who?
Abbot you don't know who this is!

Knock, knock
Who's there?
Nobel
Nobel who?
Nobel...that's why I knocked!

Knock, knock
Who's there?
Mikey
Mikey who?
Mikey doesn't fit in the keyhole!

Knock, knock
Who's there?
Viper
Viper who?
Viper nose, it's running!

Knock, knock
Who's there?
Armageddon
Armageddon who?
Armageddon a little bored.
Let's get out of here!

Knock, knock
Who's there?
Ben
Ben who?
Ben knocking for ten minutes!

Knock, knock
Who's there?
Lettuce
Lettuce who?
Lettuce in, it's cold outside!

Knock, knock
Who's there?
Cher
Cher who?
Cher would be nice if you
opened the door!

Knock, knock
Who's there?
Cabbage
Cabbage who?
You expect a cabbage to have a last name?

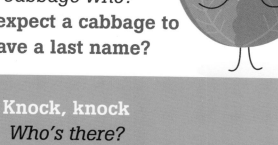

Knock, knock
Who's there?
Smellmop
Smellmop who?
Ew, no thanks!

Knock, knock
Who's there?
Opportunity
Opportunity who?
Opportunity doesn't knock twice!

Knock, knock
Who's there?
Iva
Iva who?
Iva sore hand from knocking!

Knock, knock
Who's there?
Dejah
Dejah who?
Knock, knock

Knock, knock
Who's there?
Needle
Needle who?
Needle little help right now!

Knock, knock
Who's there?
Oozy.
Oozy who?
Oozy that monster
behind you?

Knock, knock
Who's there?
Alice
Alice who?
Alice fair in love and war.

Knock, knock
Who's there?
Alex
Alex who?
Alex-plain when you open the door!

Knock, knock
Who's there?
Alex
Alex who?
Hey, Alex the questions
around here!

Knock, knock
Who's there?
Alpaca
Alpaca who?
Alpaca bag, you pack a suitcase!

Knock, knock
Who's there?
Howl
Howl who?
Howl you know unless you
open the door?

Knock, knock
Who's there?
Snow
Snow who?
Snow use. The joke is over.

Knock, knock
Who's there?
Control freak
Contro–
Okay, now you say "control freak who"?

Knock, knock
Who's there?
Donut
Donut who?
Donut ask, it's a secret!

Knock, knock
Who's there?
Kent
Kent who?
Kent you tell by the sound
of my voice?

Knock, knock
Who's there?
Orange
Orange who?
Orange you going to let me in?

Knock, knock
Who's there?
Amanda
Amanda who?
Amanda fix the door for you!

Knock, knock
Who's there?
Amy
Amy who?
Amy fraid I forgot!

Knock, knock
Who's there?
Norma Lee
Norma Lee who?
Norma Lee I don't knock on random doors,
but I had to meet you!

Knock, knock
Who's there?
Cargo
Cargo who?
Cargo beep beep!

Knock, knock
Who's there?
Billy Bob Joe Penny
Billy Bob Joe Penny who?
Really? How many Billy
Bob Joe Pennys do you know?

Knock, knock
Who's there?
Radio
Radio who?
Radio not, here I come!

Knock, knock
Who's there?
Canoe
Canoe who?
Canoe come out now?

Knock, knock
Who's there?
Sadie
Sadie who?
Sadie magic word and I'll come in!

Knock, knock
Who's there?
Dozen
Dozen who?
Dozen anyone wanna let me in?

Knock, knock
Who's there?
Beats
Beats who?
Beats me!

Knock, knock
Who's there?
Ida
Ida who?
I think it's pronounced Idaho.

Knock, knock
Who's there?
Cook
Cook who?
There's a chicken in your house??

Knock, knock
Who's there?
Etch
Etch who?
Bless you!

Knock, knock
Who's there?
Weirdo
Weirdo who?
Weirdo you think you're going?

Knock, knock
Who's there?
Dishes
Dishes who?
Dishes your mother, open up!

Knock, knock
Who's there?
Reed
Reed who?
Redo? Alright. Knock, knock

Knock, knock
Who's there?
Mustache
Mustache who?
I mustache you a question.

Knock, knock
Who's there?
Justin
Justin who?
Justin time for dinner!

Knock, knock
Who's there?
Ears
Ears who?
Ears another knock-knock joke!

Animals

What did the duck say when buying lipstick?
Put it on my bill.

What do you call a cow with no legs?
Ground beef!

Why did the kangaroo stop drinking coffee?
It got too jumpy!

How do you stop an elephant from charging?
Take away its credit cards.

Why don't dogs make good dancers?
They have two left feet.

What do you call a dog magician?
A labracadabrador!

**What did the duck say when
it dropped the dishes?**
I sure hope I didn't quack any.

What do you call a sleeping cow?
A bull-dozer!

**What happens to a frog's car
when it breaks down?**

It gets toad away.

**What do you call a chicken
at the North Pole?**

Lost!

Why did the turkey cross the road?

To prove he wasn't chicken!

What goes "ooooo"?

A cow with no lips.

Why are cats boring storytellers?

Because they only have one tail.

Why do cows never have any money?

Because the farmers milk them dry!

**What do you call a grizzly bear
caught in the rain?**

A drizzly bear!

**What do you call a cow that
just had a baby?**

Decalfinated!

Why do birds use security cameras?
To stop people from robin the birdhouse.

What kind of market should you never take a dog to?
A flea market!

Where do you send a letter to a lion?
Mane Street.

Where do sheep go on vacation?
The Baaa-hamas!

What should you do if your dog chews a dictionary?
Take the words out of his mouth.

What's a cat's favorite dessert?
Chocolate mouse.

How do horses stay in shape?
They keep a stable diet!

Why didn't the boy trust the tiger?
He thought it was a lion!

Why aren't elephants rich?
Because they work for peanuts!

Why did the elephant stay at the airport?
It was waiting for its trunk.

**What should you do when you're
tired of fish jokes?**
Scale back.

What did the mama cow say to the baby cow?
It's pasture bedtime.

What do you get from a pampered cow?
Spoiled milk!

What kinds of cars do cats like to drive?
Fur–arris.

**What did the judge say when the
skunk entered the courtroom?**
Odor in the court!

What do you call a cow with no milk?
A milk dud.

**What do you get when you cross
a chicken with a cow?**

Roost beef.

Why do cows have hooves instead of feet?

Because they lactose.

Why do cows like jokes?

Because they want to be a–moo–sed!

**What kind of ant is bigger than
an elephant?**

A gi–ant!

**Why were the elephants
kicked out of the pool?**

They kept dropping their trunks!

What do you call a lazy baby kangaroo?

A pouch potato.

What's more impressive than a talking dog?

A spelling bee.

**What's the difference between
a cat and a frog?**

*A cat has nine lives,
but a frog croaks every night!*

**What goes down but never
goes up?**
An elevator with an elephant in it.

**What did the horse say when the waiter
greeted him with "hey"?**
You read my mind!

Why do birds fly south in the winter?
Because it's too far to walk!

**Why did the poor dog chase
his own tail?**
He was trying to make both ends meet.

What do dogs and phones have in common?
They both have collar IDs.

What dog keeps the best time?
A watch dog!

Why are cats so good at video games?
Because they have nine lives!

Why was the cow afraid?
He was a cow-herd.

What does a fish do in a crisis?
Sea-kelp.

Why do pandas like old movies?
Because they play in black and white!

What was the goal of the detective duck?
To quack the case.

What's black and white and blue?
A depressed zebra.

Where do polar bears vote?
At the North Poll.

What's the best way to cook a gator?
In a croc-pot!

What do you get when you cross a cow with a hyena?
A laughing stock!

What do you get with fifteen cows and ten goats?
A lot of milk.

What does a snow shark give you?
Frost bites!

**Who fills a baby shark's
Christmas stocking?**
Santa Jaws!

Why do sharks swim in salt water?
Because pepper water makes them sneeze!

**What do you call the mushy stuff
between a shark's teeth?**
Slow swimmers.

What's a shark's favorite TV show?
Whale of Fortune!

**What happens when you cross a great
white shark with a cowfish?**
*I don't know, but I wouldn't
want to milk it.*

**What does a dog basketball coach
do before a game?**
Give the team a pup talk.

What has 4,000 eyes and 8,000 legs?
2,000 dogs.

What's a dog's favorite pizza?
Pup-peroni!

Why do cats always get their own way?
They're very purr-suasive!

What was Dracula's favorite dog?
A bloodhound.

Why did the dog quit his job?
The work was too ruff!

What did you call a small, frozen dog?
A pup-sicle!

What do you get if you cross a large boat with a small dog?
A Ship Tzu!

Why should you be careful when it's raining cats and dogs?
You might step in a poodle.

What do you get when you cross a dog with a calculator?
A friend you can count on.

**What happens when a giant lizard
makes noise in a cave?**

You hear a big gecko.

Why are cats great singers?

Because they're very meow-sical.

What do cats enjoy on a hot day?

Mice cream sundaes.

**What did the daddy snake say
to the sad baby snake?**

Stop crying and viper nose.

What do you call a cat with eight legs?

An octo-puss!

What do you call a cat that loves to bowl?

An alley cat.

**What do you get when you cross
a dairy and a duckpond?**

Cheese and quackers!

How does a dog stop a DVD?

He presses the paws button.

What do you call a rabbit with fleas?

Bugs Bunny!

Sports

**What do you call a boomerang
that doesn't work?**

A stick.

What's an insect's favorite sport?

Cricket!

**Why are hockey players good at
making friends?**

They know how to break the ice!

**What do you get when you cross a
quarterback with a carpet?**

A throw rug.

**What's the difference between a
pickpocket and an umpire?**

One steals watches and one watches steals.

**What did the baseball glove
say to the ball?**

Catch you later!

Why did the football coach go to the bank?

He wanted his quarter back!

When is a baby good at basketball?

When it's dribbling.

I kept wondering why the baseball was getting bigger...

...then it hit me.

Why is tennis such a loud sport?

The players raise a racquet.

Why do basketball players love donuts?

Because you can dunk them!

What do hockey players and magicians have in common?

They both do hat tricks.

Why did the man keep swimming the backstroke after breakfast?

He didn't want to swim on a full stomach!

Why did the soccer ball quit the team?

It was tired of being kicked around!

What's a chimney sweep's favorite sport?
Sootball.

Where do catchers sit at lunch?
Behind the plate.

Where does the majority of a hockey player's salary come from?
The tooth fairy!

Why do Canadians always beat Germans in hockey?
Canadians bring their "eh" game, while Germans bring their wurst.

How do baseball players keep up with each other?
Every once in a while, they touch base.

Why are soccer players great at math?
They know how to use their heads!

Which baseball player holds water?
The pitcher.

Why does someone who runs marathons make a good student?
Because education pays off in the long run!

Why was the basketball player sketching chickens?
The coach told her to learn how to draw fouls.

What did the skeleton drive to the hockey game?
The Zam-bony!

What do football players drink?
Penal-tea!

How do football players deal with their problems?
They tackle them head on!

Where do you keep your baseball mitt while driving?
The glove compartment.

What runs around a baseball field but never moves?
The fence.

Why did the basketball player bring his suitcase to the game?
Because he traveled a lot!

Why did the ballerina quit?

Because it was tu-tu hard!

**What animal is best at hitting
a baseball?**

A bat!

**What do pancakes and baseball teams
have in common?**

They both need a good batter.

**What kinds of stories do basketball
players tell?**

Tall tales!

When is a baseball player like a thief?

When he steals a base!

**What's harder to catch the
faster you run?**

Your breath!

What are the rules for zebra baseball?

Three stripes and you're out.

How do baseball players stay cool?

They sit next to the fans.

What's the hardest part of skydiving?

The ground!

**Why are hockey players known
for their summer teeth?**

Summer here, summer there.

**What do you call a pig that
plays basketball?**

A ball hog.

Why did the golfer wear two pairs of pants?

In case he got a hole in one!

**Why should bowling alleys
be quiet?**

So you can hear a pin drop!

Why are frogs so good at basketball?

They always make the jump shots.

**Why was the ghost asked to join
the football team?**

They needed a little spirit!

What has eighteen legs and catches flies?

A baseball team.

Why didn't the dog want to play football?
It was a boxer!

What does a baseball player and a spider have in common?
They both catch flies!

How do you start a firefly race?
Ready, set, glow!

I watched hockey before it was cool.
It was swimming. I watched swimming.

Why does a pitcher raise one leg when he throws the ball?
If he raised them both, he'd fall!

Did you hear the joke about the pop fly?
Forget it, it's way over your head.

Why are baseball games at night?
The bats sleep during the day.

What's the difference between a Yankee fan and a dentist?
One roots for the Yanks, and the other yanks for the roots.

**How do mushrooms keep track of
points in a basketball game?**
They use a sporeboard.

What's the best thing about rock climbing?
It makes you feel boulder.

Why can't you see a Super Bowl LIVE?
Because "E" is not a Roman numeral.

Why are hockey rinks round?
*Because if they were 90 degrees,
the ice would melt!*

What lights up a soccer stadium?
A soccer match!

**How many golfers does it take to
change a lightbulb?**
Fore!

How does an eagle practice for volleyball?
*She doesn't practice.
She prefers to wing it.*

What is a rainstorm's favorite type of sled?
De-luge.

Science

What did the femur say to the patella?
I kneed you!

Why don't people like anatomy jokes?
They're too cornea!

**Why did the physicist break up
with the biologist?**
There was no chemistry!

**What did the left hand say to the
other hand?**
How are you always right?

Why do surgeons make so much money?
They always get their cut.

Why do chemists like nitrates?
They are cheaper than day rates!

Why is the nose in the middle of your face?
Because it's the scenter!

Where does criminal light end up?
In prism.

What has thirteen hearts but no organs?
A deck of cards.

What do you find inside a clean nose?
Fingerprints!

**What's the difference between a dog
and a marine biologist?**
One wags a tail, and the other tags a whale.

Why is the ocean so salty?
The land never waves back!

**What did the cell say say to its sister
when it bumped its foot?**
Mitosis!

Where do hippos go to study medicine?
The hippocampus.

What do you do with a chemist who is sick?
*First, you try helium. Then, you try curium.
But if that fails, you have to barium.*

**How much room do fungi
need to grow?**

As mushroom as possible!

**What did one tectonic plate say when
it bumped into another?**

Sorry, my fault!

**What will never go viral no matter
how popular they get?**

Antibiotics.

**Why did the chemist hang up periodic
table posters everywhere?**

*It made him feel like he was
in his element.*

**What did the balloon say
to the doctor?**

I feel light-headed.

**What's the quickest way to a
man's heart?**

Through his chest!

Why does the brain use cosmetics?

To make up its mind!

What's the matter?
Solid, liquid, or gas.

Who's shorter than a biologist?
A microbiologist!

What is a nuclear physicist's favorite snack?
Fission chips!

**What do you call a tower made
of body parts?**
Body building.

Why did the brain refuse to take a bath?
It didn't want to be brainwashed.

Why don't fossils like scary movies?
Because they're petrified!

**Have you heard of the new book
about helium?**
It's impossible to put down!

Want to hear a joke about potassium?
K.

Anyone know jokes about sodium?
Na.

Why can't you trust atoms?
They make up everything.

Why did the germ cross the microscope?
To get to the other slide.

How did the doctor cure the invisible man?
She took him to the ICU!

Did you know that legs are hereditary?
They run in your jeans!

What did the parasite say when it wasn't seated at the restaurant?
Well, you're not a very good host.

Why did the brain go out for a run?
It wanted to jog its memory!

Why are eyes considered to be the last organ to die?
Because pupils die-late!

Why did the student fail anatomy?
Because his teacher was really sternum.

What unit of measurement do you use to weigh bones?
Skele-tons!

What's the least honest bone in the body?
The fibula.

What did one nostril say to the other?
You think you're better than me, but it snot true!

Einstein developed a theory about space.
It was about time, too.

Why are skeletons so calm?
Nothing gets under their skin.

Do you know the name Pavlov?
It rings a bell.

Why is geology the best science?
It rocks!

How often should you tell element jokes?
Periodically.

What did one DNA strand say to the other?
Do these genes look good on me?

Why were the atoms such great friends?
They bonded well together!

What do you call the rear door of a cafeteria?
Bacteria!

Why is it so hard to wake up in the morning?
Newton's First Law: A body at
rest wants to stay at rest.

What did the radio say when the
music was turned up too loud?
Ouch! That hertz my ears!

What do you call a flying organ?
A gull bladder.

Which side of a human has the most hair?
The outside.

What did one lung say to the other?
I'll always be th-air for you!

Why did the nurse have a red pen?
In case she needed to draw blood!

What do you call a diver
wearing earplugs?
I SAID, WHAT DO YOU CALL A DIVER
WEARING EARPLUGS.

What did one volcano say
to the other volcano?
I lava you!

What did the diamond say to the ruby?
Nothing. Minerals don't talc!

How does a geologist chill out?
In a rocking chair.

What do you get when you put granite in the Atlantic Ocean?
Wet granite.

How do you confuse coal miners?
Give them two shovels and ask them to take their pick!

What do protons and optimists have in common?
They know how to stay positive.

What do dentists call their X-rays?
Tooth-pics.

What did the limestone say to the geologist?
Don't take me for granite!

What shape is the DNA that makes up chewing gum?
A bubble helix.

**What happens to grapes when
you step on them?**
They wine!

Why were the apples and oranges alone?
The banana split.

What do you call two banana peels?
A pair of slippers.

What kind of apple has a short temper?
A crab apple!

How do you measure the weight of crackers?
In grahams.

Why did the apple pie cross the road?
It saw a fork up ahead.

Why are oranges the fastest fruit?
They never run out of juice!

What do you call a bunch of strawberries playing instruments together?
A jam session.

What's a scarecrow's favorite fruit?
Straw-berries!

What do you call a cat who eats lemons?
A sourpuss.

What did the lemon say to the lime?
Sour you doing?

Did you hear about the fruit that gave people a warm fuzzy feeling?
It was a real peach!

Why did the butcher work overtime at the shop?
To make ends meat.

What did the mama tomato say when her child was falling behind on their walk?
Ketchup!

**Why did the cantaloupe jump into
the swimming pool?**

He wanted to be a watermelon!

How do you make a lemon drop?

Just let it fall.

**What did the grape say to
the peanut butter?**
'Tis the season to be jelly!

What do you call a gourmet omelet?

Eggs-cellent!

Why was the cookie crying?

Because his mom was a wafer so long.

Where do baby apes sleep?

In apricots.

What is black, white, green, and bumpy?

A pickle in a tuxedo!

What kind of fruit can fix your sink?

A PLUM-ber.

**What happens when you're mean
to chickpeas?**

They falafel.

What's blue and goes up and down?

A blueberry on a pogo stick.

**What do you get when
1,000 blueberries try to go through
a door at the same time?**

A blueberry jam.

How fast does milk go?

Pasteurize before you know it.

**What did the blueberry pie say
to the pecan pie?**

You're nuts!

Why was the peach late for work?

It had to make a pit stop on the way.

Why couldn't the banana yell high?

It could only yellow.

How do you make a strawberry shake?

Put it in the freezer!

Why don't bananas snore when they sleep?

So they don't wake up the rest of the bunch.

Why are butchers so funny?

They always ham it up!

What kind of desserts does a turkey like?

Peach gobbler.

What is yellow on the inside and green on the outside?

A banana dressed up as a zucchini.

Why do elephants paint their toenails red?

So they can hide in cherry trees.

Have you ever seen an elephant in a cherry tree?

(Wait for a "No" response.)
Works, doesn't it?!

Why was the apple uncomfortable in the fruit bowl?

Pear pressure.

Why did the orange go out with the prune?

Because it couldn't find a date!

How many apples grow on a tree?
All of them!

Why did the tomato blush?
Because it saw the salad dressing.

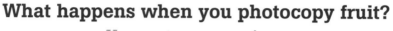

Why did the banana visit the doctor?
It wasn't peeling well!

What happens when you photocopy fruit?
You get a paper jam.

What did the fruit say to his valentine?
I love you from my head tomato!

How do you make an apple turnover?
Push it down the hill.

**If there are three oranges and
four apples in your hand,
what do you have?**
Very large hands!

**What did the banana say to
the elephant?**
Nothing. Bananas can't talk.

What do you give to a sick lemon?

Lemon aid!

Why did the bulb pack an apple in his bag?

He wanted to have a light snack.

Wanna hear a joke about pizza?

Never mind, it's too cheesy.

Why did the apple pie go to the dentist!

Because it needed a filling!

How do you fix a broken tomato?

Use tomato paste!

What did the watermelon say to the cantaloupe?

You're one in a melon!

What did bacon say to tomato?

Lettuce get together!

Why did the students eat their homework?

Because the teacher said it was a piece of cake.

**Why is it so difficult to work
at an apple pie factory?**

They have such a high turnover rate!

Why did the can crusher quit his job?

Because it was soda pressing.

**What do you call a round, green vegetable
that breaks out of prison?**

An escapea.

Why does yogurt love going to museums?

Because it's cultured.

What do you call a fake noodle?

An impasta.

**What's orange and sounds
like a parrot?**

A carrot.

**What did the fisherman say
to the magician?**

Pick a cod...any cod!

Why were the two cheeses identical?

They were cut from the same mold!

**What do you call a corn cob
that joins the army?**

Kernel!

**What do you call an apple that
plays the saxophone?**

A tooty fruity.

How did the hipsters burn their mouths?

By eating pizza before it was cool.